I feel...

 happy
 calm
 sad
 angry
 worried
 confident

 scared
 surprised
 disgusted
 unsure
 excited
 embarrassed

 panicked
 focused
 disappointed
 silly
 friendly
 jealous

 bored
 muddled
 tired
 unwell
 hungry
 hot or cold

How do I say "I feel confident" in Makaton?

I feel

Take one hand with your thumb and middle finger pointing to your face and lift your hand up and say, "I feel".

confident.

With a confident look on your face, place one hand across your chest and make a 'C' shape with your hand and say, "confident".

ISBN 978-1-78270-694-6

Copyright © Channon Gray

All rights reserved. No part of this publication may be reproduced or utilised in any form or by any means electronic or mechanical, including photocopying, recording, or by any information storage and retrieval system now known or hereafter invented, without the prior written permission of the publisher and copyright holder.

No part of this book may be used or reproduced in any manner for the purpose of training artificial intelligence technologies or systems. In accordance with Article 4(3) of the DSM Directive 2019/790, Award Publications Limited expressly reserves this work from the text and data mining exception.

First published 2026

Published by Award Publications Limited
The Old Riding School, Welbeck, Worksop, S80 3LR

awardpublications @award.books
www.awardpublications.co.uk

25-1206 1

Printed in China

All About Confident Scribble

Written and illustrated by
Channon Gray

award

Confidence is believing in yourself, inside and out.

Ahem! I am Confident Scribble.

It is a feeling that is powerful and worth talking about.

When we are confident,
we pick ourselves up when we fall.

Confidence happens when we know we are enough...

I am enough!

...just as we are.

Confidence feels like a BIG cheer!

Knowing it will be okay and you have nothing to fear.

Growing our confidence isn't about being perfect.

It's learning each day,
because mistakes are all part of it!

Hooray! I am Elated Scribble.

Being confident looks and feels different for everyone.

It can help you try new things and have lots of fun!

Confidence can feel like a **warm** and **fuzzy** feeling inside.

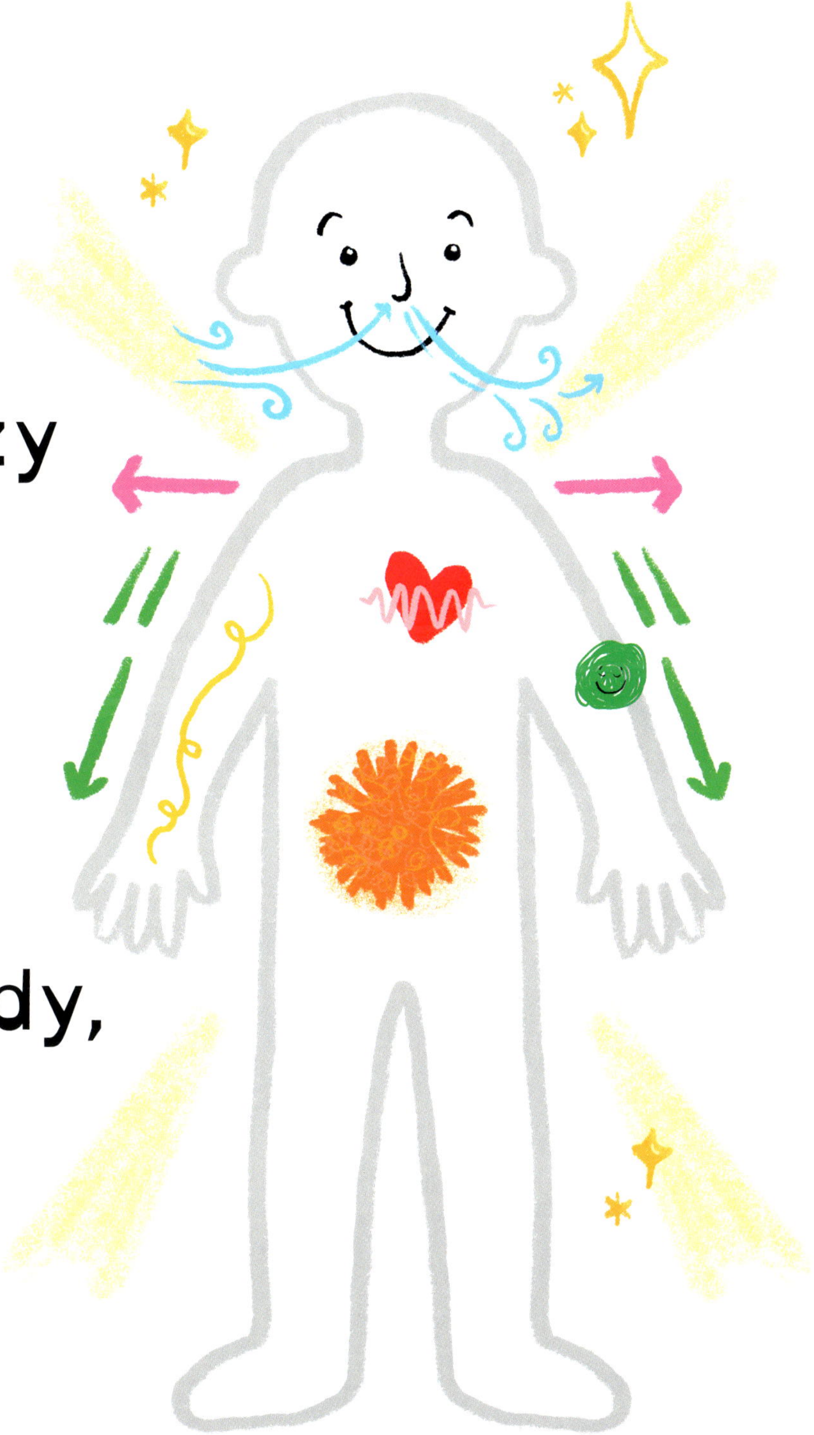

Our heart **beat** is **steady,** our muscles r e l a x and our shoulders feel w i d e.

Feeling confident can help us to try again after we make a mistake.

Because every new try

helps us to learn,

even if sometimes we need a little break.

When we feel confident, we can manage BIG feelings better and feel proud of what we can do.

We believe in ourselves,
and we'll always find a way through.

Being confident isn't about being the loudest, or boastful – or even the star.

It's trying your best on the inside and out, just being who you are.

Confidence can be quiet...

squeeeeaakkk...

...or confidence can be Loud!

ROOAARR!

It's the courage to be yourself, not hide behind a cloud.

Gaining confidence is like a seed, growing over time.
Slow at first, but when encouraged,
see it start to climb.

Storms may knock us back and fill us with self-doubt.
But nurturing your confidence will always make it sprout.

Positive self-talk
is like a friend who
whispers in your ear:

"You can do it!"

This takes away our fear.

With positive self-talk, we feel the power inside.

"I am capable."
"I can do tricky things."
"I do not need to hide."

When we are confident,
we have a secret superpower.

The power of

YET

helps us grow
and flower.

I can't do it **YET**,

but that's okay.

I'll keep on learning
and know I'll get better each day.

When challenges come,
we can't just run away.

Stop, pause and breathe!
I am Stop Scribble.

We may be scared,
but trying our best,
we will find a way.

We think it through
and give it a go.

And with every try,
our inner confidence grows.

Sob, sob!
I am Sad Scribble.

Uhh! I am
Worried Scribble.

Sometimes, people can be unkind.

"I could do that better than you."

"Shhh! Go away!"

"Pfft! I am Jealous Scribble."

"Grr! I am Angry Scribble."

"NO!"

"I am not ok with this!"

We need to be confident to share what is on our mind.

When we stand up for ourselves,
and don't back down.

We stand up tall and wear our confidence crown.

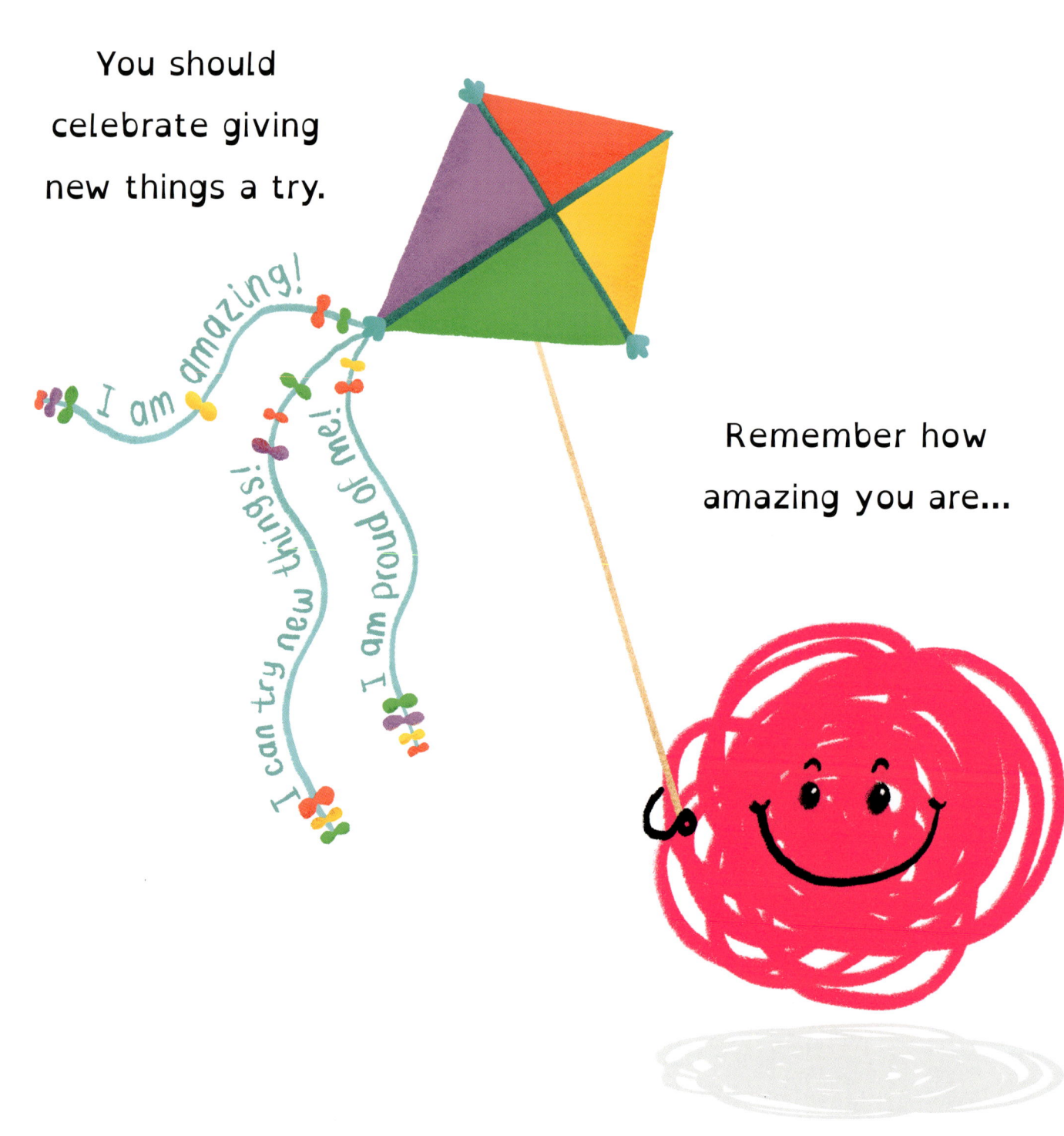

Sometimes, feeling confident can be tough.

But when things feel tricky or difficult, say aloud:

"I know I am enough!"

Confidence might feel strange and new, but it **grows** with each and every thing we do.

You'll always find it deep inside and in the words you speak.

Confident Scribble Activities

Decorate an old sheet to make a 'Confidence Cape'. Write on it things you are proud of. Wear it like a superhero!

Practise your superhero stance – hands on hips, arms wide, standing tall. This is your 'Power Pose'.

Look in the mirror and say three kind things to yourself aloud, like, "I can try again." Try using a funny voice!

The Scribbles Crew love to see your creations! Ask your grown-ups to share them on social media using #TheScribblesCrew

Scan the QR code on the back cover for more great Scribbles Crew activities, sing-along songs and teaching resources specially created by The Exciting Teacher.

www.thescribblescrew.com